A Special Gift

_____

_____

_____

_____

_____

With Love,

_____

_____

date

Look for these other *Hugs*™ books:

Hugs for Coffee Lovers
Hugs for Dad
Hugs for Daughters
Hugs for Friends
Hugs for Friends, Book 2
Hugs for Grads
Hugs for Girlfriends
Hugs for Grandparents
Hugs for Heroes
Hugs for the Holidays
Hugs for the Hurting
Hugs for Your Birthday
Hugs for Pet Lovers

Hugs for Kids
Hugs for Mom
Hugs for New Moms
Hugs for Nurses
Hugs for Sisters
Hugs for Sons
Hugs for Teachers
Hugs for Teens
Hugs for Mom, Book 2
Hugs for Brothers
Hugs for Those in Love
Hugs for Women
Hugs for Women on the Go
Hugs to Encourage and Inspire

Stories, sayings, and scriptures to encourage and inspire the...

hugs™

for
Grandma

CHRYS HOWARD

Personalized Scriptures by
LEANN WEISS

HOWARD
PUBLISHING CO.

Our purpose at Howard Publishing is to:

- *Increase faith* in the hearts of growing Christians
- *Inspire holiness* in the lives of believers
- *Instill hope* in the hearts of struggling people everywhere

Because He's coming again!

Hugs for Grandma © 2001 by Chrys Howard
All rights reserved. Printed in the United States of America

Published by Howard Publishing Co., Inc.
3117 North 7th Street, West Monroe, LA 71291-2227

05 06 07 08 09 10   21 20 19 18 17

Personalized scriptures by LeAnn Weiss, owner of Encouragement
Company, 3006 Brandywine Dr., Orlando, FL 32806; 407-898-4410

Edited by Philis Boultinghouse
Interior design by LinDee Loveland

Library of Congress Cataloging-in-Publication Data

Howard, Chrys, 1953–
    Hugs for grandma : stories, sayings, and scriptures to encourage
    and inspire the [heart] / Chrys Howard ; personalized scriptures by
    LeAnn Weiss.
        p. cm.
    ISBN 1-58229-154-3
    1. Grandmothers—Religious life. 2. Grandparent and child—
    Religious aspects—Christianity. I. Weiss, LeAnn. II. Title.

BV4528.5 .H69 2001
242'.6431—dc21

                                                    00-046107

Scripture quotations taken from the Holy Bible, New International Version, © 1973, 1978, 1984 International Bible Society. Used by permis-
sion of Zondervan Bible Publishers; and the Holy Bible, New King James
Version, © 1982 by Thomas Nelson, Inc.

I love you!

I dedicate this book to my grandmothers,
Myrtle Anne Durham and *Lela May Shackelford*,
who inspired, encouraged, and entertained me through my childhood.

I thank God for my mother, *Betty Jo Shackelford*,
and my mother-in-law, *Mamie Jean Howard*,
who did the same for my children.

Now, I pray that I will continue the legacy of loving unconditionally
to my grandchildren, who make each day an adventure.
John Luke, Sadie, Macy, Asa, Ally,
Will, Maddox, Aslyn, and *Bella* —

I love you!

Contents

vii

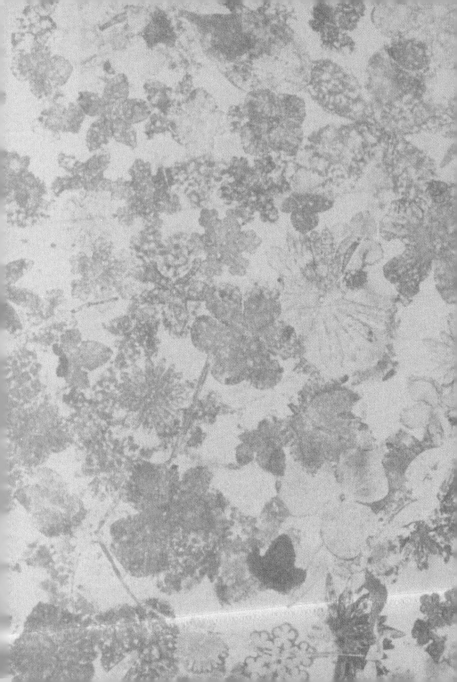

You Are
Called

Answer
the Call

$\mathcal{I}$'ve redeemed you and called you by name. I'll never abandon you in your search for Me. My name is 100 percent trustworthy. I love to do far beyond all that you can ask or dream according to My power, which is at work in your family even when you don't realize it.

Dreaming for you,

Your God of Abundant Life

—from Isaiah 43:1; Psalm 9:10; Ephesians 3:20

$Grandmothers,$ thank you for being flexible about your "grandma" name.

Grandmothers are among the few people on earth who are content to be called anything someone else decides. People are fairly picky about their names, aren't they? No one likes to see her name misspelled in print. We cringe when we hear it mispronounced. We roll our eyes when we are called by someone else's name.

The dictionary tells us that a name is that by which a person or thing is designated. Psychologists tell us that calling someone by his or her name builds self-esteem and gives a feeling of importance. School-teachers tell us that they strive to learn their students' names quickly in order to help each child feel special and noticed. Children tell us it bothers them when their parents can't remember their names, listing the whole family before their own name is called.

But, grandmothers, you have risen above the name game. You have learned a great lesson from Jesus—Messiah, Lamb of God, Son of Man, Lord. Do you recognize these names? Of course you do. They are the names used to call on our Savior, Jesus. Each

name contributes something unique and con-
jures up a different image or perspective of Jesus.
And there are many more names for this one man,
Jesus. Jesus invites us to call on his name often—in
times of joy and in times of sorrow—and he never
tires of hearing our calls.

What do your grandchildren call you? I would sus-
pect that whatever it is, you are thrilled with it. I'm
sure something special happened when you became
Mimi, Nana, G-Mom, or Mamaw. Maybe it was something you said or did, or maybe it was just the name
that past generations in your family have used. In
any case, you all have your own story. And, just like
Jesus, you don't really mind which name you are
called.

Your grandchildren could call you anything,
and you would have answered. You are that
special person who will always answer when
they call, always listen when they speak,
and always love them no matter what
they do. You are their grandmother.
And just like Jesus, you invite them
to call on you whenever they
want, and you will never tire
of hearing your name.

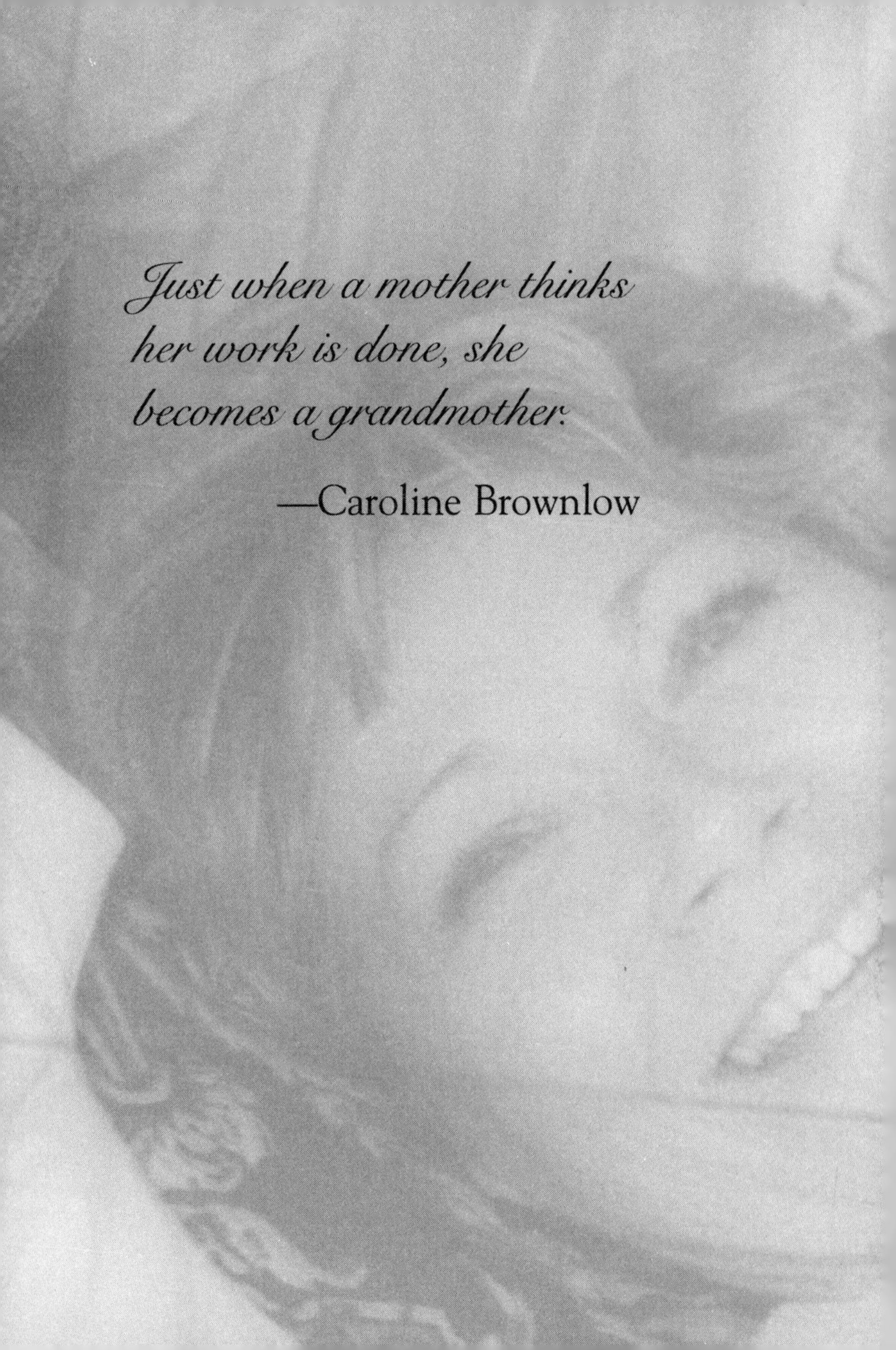

*Just when a mother thinks
her work is done, she
becomes a grandmother.*

—Caroline Brownlow

Being a mother was what Stacy wanted most in her life.

An Answered Prayer

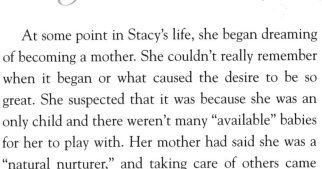

At some point in Stacy's life, she began dreaming of becoming a mother. She couldn't really remember when it began or what caused the desire to be so great. She suspected that it was because she was an only child and there weren't many "available" babies for her to play with. Her mother had said she was a "natural nurturer," and taking care of others came easily to her.

Sometimes her mother had wished Stacy weren't so caring. Cats and dogs and little pink pigs all made their way into Stacy's heart. And because Stacy was an only child with no hope for siblings, her mom generally said yes to every animal she wanted. Although she wanted to draw the line after she found Stacy bathing the pig in her bathtub, she didn't. Friends called their house a "zoo for a day."

But being a mother was what Stacy wanted most in her life. She had longed to feel the soft, tender touch of her own baby's hand, to change diapers and make bottles. Her friends used to say, "Stacy, get a life. You don't want to do that stuff until you have to!" They didn't understand. Stacy really thought she was ready. Even her mother didn't understand. She and her mother had always had a close relationship until that terrible day.

Stacy had tried to keep it a secret. Young girls just didn't have babies out of wedlock during the sixties. Well, of course, they did. But no one knew it. Everything was kept quiet. Girls were suddenly sent off to

visit relatives in California or sent away to "summer camp." Even if someone suspected the truth, no one talked about it. Although it is just as wrong to have sex outside of marriage today as it was in the sixties, people today seem more understanding and supportive of the choices a young girl might make. In the sixties, it was out of the question to have a baby and not be married. Raising a child alone was rarely considered.

"Stacy, this decision is for your good, sweetheart. You're only sixteen. You have your whole life ahead of you." Her mother said those words through tears and sobs so violent that Stacy was afraid her mother would never stop. "You can't take care of a baby. You have no job, no education. What would you do?" And her mom just kept quoting a scripture in Proverbs about trusting God. At the time, Stacy wasn't sure who to trust. The advice she kept hearing wasn't what she wanted to hear.

But Stacy really had no choice. It was the late sixties, and even though the world was in a sexual revolution, her parents were not. And neither was the rest of her family. There was nothing to do except put the baby up for adoption.

As Stacy grew up and older, she eventually came to terms with her mother's lack of ability to make things better. But at the time, she couldn't understand her mother. This woman had always "fixed" everything for her, but she couldn't fix this.

The day Stacy signed the adoption papers was the saddest day of her life. Her mother had to hold her hand to steady it so she could get her signature on the appropriate line. Her eyes were so heavy and so tired from crying she could barely see what she was writing. She had prayed that it was only a bad dream and that she would soon wake up.

But it wasn't a dream. *How could one night cause such pain? How could I have been so foolish? I thought Jeff truly loved me and would always be there for me!* Stacy learned a valuable lesson in one night: Appearances can be deceiving.

So much has happened since that day, Stacy thought. But Stacy was as nervous today as she had been thirty-two years ago. Only this time, it was a "happy" nervous. She was on her way to meet her baby girl. She knew she wasn't a baby anymore, but she couldn't help but think of her that way—she had no other memories of her. She hoped new memories would soon be made.

An Answered Prayer

When the phone rang exactly three weeks, one day, and six hours ago, Stacy knew the missing piece of her "life puzzle" was being nudged into place. Her life puzzle had been almost perfect; she would never deny that. Her husband, Kevin, had loved and supported her for twenty-eight years. She had worked for many years in local Christian ministries, and in the past ten years, she had spoken openly about the baby girl she had given up. She had counseled countless young girls in the same situation. Well, she always hesitated to say "the same" because every situation is unique. Certainly the times have changed, and young women have more options today. But that's one reason Stacy decided to be more vocal. She never wanted abortion to be one of those options. Even though she didn't get to raise her baby, she cherished the thought that she was alive and growing and clung to the hope of their reunion.

Although Stacy had many happy times in her life, there was a very sad part. She and Kevin had never had a child. Her desire and dream to be a mother had never become a reality.

You Are Called—*Answer the Call*

Although she had lots of "babies," as she always referred to her kindergarten students, Stacy never again felt the touch of her own newborn—not since March 13, 1968, when she kissed her baby girl good-bye.

Stacy knew she was a great teacher. Year after year parents requested her classroom for their children. And she knew she had impacted so many little lives. And she trusted God. She wasn't going to be bitter. But there were days, she had to admit, when she wanted to know why. *Why couldn't I have another baby?*

Road construction for the next four miles. Don't they realize I've got a baby to meet! Of course, they don't! Life just keeps going on. I'm seeing my baby for the first time in thirty-two years, and the road still has to be fixed! And bills must be paid, yards must be mowed, and a million other significantly insignificant things have to happen. But nothing will come between my child and me...this time.

Stacy saw a small, neat, white frame house. The yard had been freshly mowed, and the garden was full of new petunias—all waiting to welcome company. Flowing softly in the breeze were pink balloons that Stacy later discovered numbered thirty-two—one for each year Stacy and her baby had been separated. She pulled into the driveway, turned off the key, put the car in park, and automatically began praying. *Dear God, thank you for this day. Bless us and grant us peace as we begin this new relationship.*

As her eyes opened, so did the door of the house. Out stepped Jenna—the most beautiful young woman she had ever seen. Trembling, Stacy managed to get out of the car. It was an experience she knew she would hardly be able to describe to her husband. He had elected to stay at home so her emotions could be hers alone. With every part of her body, she felt as she had felt when she gave birth to this little girl. Not the pain part—just the love part. How she had wanted her! How she had cried when she knew she couldn't keep her. How she had struggled each year just to get through March 13, knowing her child was blowing out candles and opening presents, and she would never see her do those things.

The reunion was going perfectly—pictures had been exchanged, and hugs had been given until their arms hurt. Stacy was realistic and knew that some tough times would come. Questions must be asked, and answers must be given. But for today, so far, everything was perfect. And the best part was meeting Micah and Meagen, her grandchildren. She was a grandmother!

When Jenna had told her over the phone that she had grandchildren, a new set of tears began to flow. *Finally a baby to cuddle!* Actually, Jenna had told Stacy that her children were the reason she had tracked Stacy down. Jenna's adoptive mother had died of ovarian cancer three years earlier, and Jenna longed for her children to have the love of a grandmother. But truth be known, Jenna also longed for the love of a mother. Someone to share pictures with and pack a suitcase for and have lunch with. Someone to share her life with. Finding her birth mother seemed the perfect solution.

Stacy couldn't have been happier when Jenna finally said the words Stacy had waited so long to hear: "Can I call you Mama?"

"Yes," came Stacy's quick reply. "I've waited so long to hear you say that word!" Jenna picked up

Micah, who had just turned two. Meagen, only six months old, had already snuggled up to her new grandmother.

"Micah, I want you to know that this is my mama, and that she is your grandmother—yours and Meagen's," Stacy said softly.

Micah's two-year-old brain went to work, and he quickly responded: "If she's your mama, then she's my two-mama!"

Jenna laughed and explained, "Ever since I had Meagen, I've said so many times how I have two babies. Now he thinks he's met another mama. We can work on another grandmother name if you want us to."

"Of course not! It's perfect. As a matter of fact, I can't wait to share this with my friends."

After all these years of waiting to be a mama, Stacy was delighted to be someone's "two-mama." All of her friends who were now grandparents had spent hours deciding what they wanted their grand-children to call them, and this little guy had figured out Stacy's name in one

minute. Stacy had never heard it used before. She knew her friends would be jealous of such a special name. "I wonder if it's legal to copyright a name?" she joked to Jenna.

Appearances certainly can be deceiving, Stacy thought, as she drove away from the little white house with thirty-two pink balloons. *I began this day as Stacy—no children, but now I'm Stacy—Jenna's mama and Meagen and Micah's two-mama. What a double blessing!*

"Trust in the Lord with all your heart and lean not on your own understanding." Thank you, God, for answering my prayers, and thank you, Mom, for reminding me often of that scripture.

What special memories do you have of being "called" by your grandchildren?

_____

_____

_____

_____

_____

_____

_____

_____

_____

_____

_____

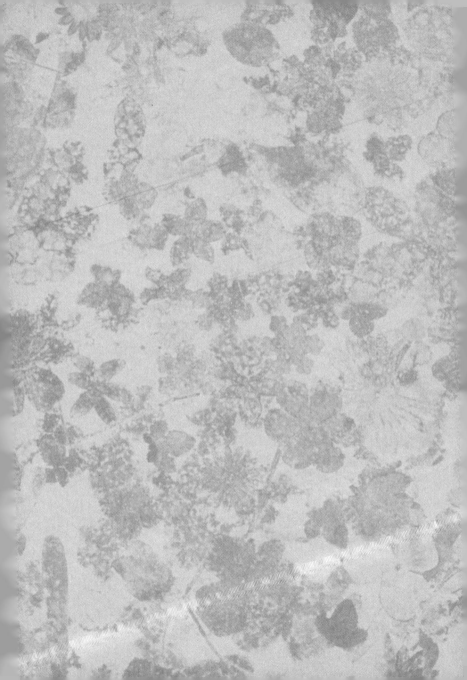

You Have
a Gift

Give It

*Y*ou're a special part of My family, sharing My treasures. Be a faithful steward of everything I've entrusted to you. When you give, you'll bountifully receive beyond your initial gift. Remember, love is the gift that holds everything together in perfect unity.

Extravagantly,

Your God of Every Good
and Perfect Gift

—from Romans 8:17; 1 Corinthians 4:2; Luke 6:38;
Colossians 3:14; James 1:17

$Grandmothers$ are notorious for wanting to lavish gifts on their grandchildren. Lavishing gifts on a grandchild is a grandmother's right, many would say. But there is the question of "spoiling" them. A wise grandmother once said, "It's not what you give a child that spoils them; it's what you allow them to do with it that does the damage."

Even so, you must remember that the greatest gifts are not bought at Toys "R" Us. They aren't found on the shopping channel, and you can't charge them on your MasterCard. Oh, bicycles and baby dolls are nice. But there is something more precious and actually more costly.

Do you realize that the future of homemade biscuits rests with you? Only you have the secret knowledge of knowing where to look for a rainbow after the rain has stopped. And then there's the ability to decide what size container will best hold a lizard, a frog, and four leaves. And who knows better than a grandmother how to rock a baby to sleep or to fold a blanket to custom fit a tiny newborn?

And the best gift of all is your ability to love unconditionally.

inspirational message

Grandmothers, your age and wisdom have taught you to love with expectations but without conditions. You can look at the face of a grandchild and not see a dirty-faced kid with too much energy; rather, you see the future. Your vision is sharpening with age. "When others see a shepherd boy, God may see a king," so the song by Ray Boltz goes. You, like God, see the potential, yet you do not apply the pressure. You are content to watch as if waiting for that first flower to bloom in spring, knowing that the bloom will come in time.

These are the best gifts, aren't they? What's the price? Maybe a Saturday morning when homemade biscuits are ordered by hungry teens or a summer evening waiting for the rain to stop. Perhaps it will cost you much-needed sleep when you are assigned late-night duty tending a fussy newborn.

Most of all, it will cost you your heart, given to those you love the most. There's not a grandchild alive who wouldn't want to receive these gifts. So go ahead! Lavish all you want. Your gifts will reap eternal rewards!

The best gifts are tied with heartstrings.

—Jo Petty

The instructions for the grandkids had been to
arrive at midnight with ladders, decorations,
and glue guns.

The Gift

Okay, I'm almost seventy, Betty sighed, as she locked the office door for the evening, *and I'm feeling every minute of it*. Betty Shackelford, a strong woman, whose Southern manners would never allow her to show her problems, was just plain tired! Although she couldn't understand how her mother's picture got on her new driver's license, she actually looked great for sixty-eight and enjoyed good health.

But three years ago, at a time when her friends were retiring and relaxing, Betty and her husband of forty-five years decided to open a real-estate business. So Betty became the office manager.

You Have a Gift—*Give It*

Just as they had hoped, the business flourished. Betty's job was very demanding, and when she wasn't too tired, she sometimes snickered a little and patted herself on the back at the thought that she'd never worked a day in her life until she was sixty-four years old. Well, outside the home, that is!

After all, she had raised six kids. There was bound to be some management experience in that job. As a matter of fact, Betty really looked at managing the business office just as she had her home: "Stay on a schedule, and do everything in love" was her motto. So far, it had worked.

But as Betty closed the office that particular night, she was even too tired to go to her grandson, Jake's, basketball game. And that wasn't like Betty. It was Jake's senior year, and she never missed a game. But tonight she just couldn't make it.

 Betty knew the phone would be ringing about the time she dozed off to sleep, so she willed herself to read one more page as she waited, patiently. *It's great to have so much family around*, she thought, *but you can't get away with any-*

thing. And sure enough, just before ten o'clock, the first phone call came.

"Mom, you okay?" her oldest daughter asked. "You weren't at the game."

"I'm just a little tired," was the reply. "I guess with the office work and trying to get ready for Christmas, I overdid it a little. I'll be all right tomorrow." She repeated her story three more times as kids and grandkids called to check on "Mamaw."

Now for some much-needed sleep, Betty thought as she closed her eyes. But rest escaped her. She mentally went through the checklist for the next day: Get the new house listings to the newspaper; take pictures of the house on Lakeland Drive; take a shower gift by Joneal's house; go to Jake's game; decorate the office.

Decorate the office! Now that's something I really don't have time to do! She almost cried as a feeling of being totally overwhelmed engulfed her. "No, I can do it," she said out loud.

"What's wrong?" said her husband, Luther, who was awakened from a peaceful sleep.

"Oh nothing, go back to sleep," Betty said. "I was just working on tomorrow."

You Have a Gift—*Give It*

"Why don't you work on tomorrow when tomorrow gets here?" Luther replied as he rolled over and went back to sleep.

Easy for you to say, Betty thought. *What was that little phrase my mother used to say, "A woman's work is never…"?* She finally fell asleep.

The next morning, Betty was ready to tackle the day. Well, mentally she was. But her back didn't feel right. She must have pulled something when she picked up Sadie the day before. Her granddaughter, Korie, had surprised her at the office with her two-year-old daughter, Sadie. Betty and Sadie had become best buddies. Sadie's deep dimples, dark brown eyes, and bubbling personality made her a great-grandmother's dream, and she loved to run and jump into Mamaw's waiting arms.

"I may have to hold off on decorating the office," Betty told Luther. "I seem to have pulled a muscle. I think Sadie has put on a pound or two."

"No problem," said Luther. "You'll get it done."

Easy for you to say, Betty thought.

Betty finished getting ready for work and was out the door by seven-thirty. She had just a few stops she wanted to make before she headed to the office. She knew that once she got there, she probably wouldn't get to leave until dark. *Thank goodness Wal-Mart never closes. How did we ever get our errands run before all-night shopping?* Betty wondered. Another stop for gas, and Betty was off to work.

She rounded the corner of Thomas and Arkansas Road, thankful that she lived in a small town. Many days Betty thought that if she had to fight big-city traffic, it might be enough to put her over that proverbial "edge."

As Betty pulled into the parking lot of Shackelford-French Real Estate, she was shocked to see that even in broad daylight, white twinkle lights sparkled on the bushes that surrounded her office. The tall white columns that seemed to guard the front door had been transformed into giant candy canes. Wreaths had been placed in each window, and a "Have a Merry Christmas" welcome mat warmed the entrance.

Betty slowly got out of her car. Her eyes were as bright as a child's on Christmas morning, and her hands flew

You Have a Gift—*Give It*

to cover her mouth. She carefully opened the front door and was greeted by a small, fully decorated Christmas tree, a basket filled with candy canes, and a card that read, "Mamaw, we hope you enjoy this holiday surprise. Thank you for always making Christmas special for us. We love you, your grandchildren."

Betty had not realized that Korie had come by the office the day before to "case the joint," as she later told her. She had been hard at work organizing her brothers, sisters, and cousins to give a gift that she knew her mamaw truly needed.

The instructions for the grandkids had been to arrive at midnight with ladders, decorations, and glue guns. Two hours and many laughs later, the gift was finished, and nine very excited grandchildren drove away and eagerly waited for the phone calls to come the next day.

Betty was touched almost beyond words. But she managed to leave nine messages that day that said, "Thank you, my grandchildren. There's not a better gift you could have given me."

And for some reason, Betty's back didn't seem to bother her so much that day.

Record for future generations a special memory of a gift-giving or gift-receiving time with your grandchildren.

_____

_____

_____

_____

_____

_____

_____

_____

_____

_____

You Are a
Cheerleader

Keep
Cheering

© Photography by Lamar

*Y*our words have amazing, life-giving power! Encourage your loved ones and build them up daily as you each run with endurance the race I've custom-tailored for you. Remember, I'm your rest stop, surrounding you with victory songs! You can do all things because I strengthen you. Even failure can't separate you from My unconditional love for you.

Rooting for you,
Your God

—from Proverbs 18:21;
1 Thessalonians 5:11; Hebrews 12:1–3;
Psalm 32:7; Philippians 4:13;
Romans 8:35

Have you read Hebrews 12 lately? Go ahead, read it. What better visual image could there be than the thunderous roar of a crowd cheering a runner on to victory? And the great news is that it's more than a visual image—it's reality! The Hebrews writer states: "Therefore, since we are surrounded by such a great cloud of witnesses, let us throw off everything that hinders and the sin that so easily entangles, and let us run with perseverance the race marked out for us." As a grandmother, you understand the race the Hebrews writer was talking about— the race of life. Perhaps you're right in the middle of it, or maybe you're nearing the end. In any case, you understand. When Hebrews 12 was written, the readers needed encouragement to stay strong in the face of persecution. They were called to follow the perfect example of Jesus. To encourage them, the Hebrews writer told them that many, many had gone before them and were cheering them on to victory.

While you certainly don't face the same kind or degree of persecution faced during biblical days, you do realize the difficulties and joys involved in completing the race. And we all need encouragement, don't we? We all need someone to cheer us on— someone who has already been there, right where we are now—someone who has crossed the finish line! Those who've run the race before you know your struggles, they understand the sacrifices you make, and they can truly feel your pain.

Grandmas, your grandchildren are just entering the race. And it's a race that is bigger than the Olympics, more strenuous than a Grand-Slam event, and more challenging than the Super Bowl. They're entering the race of life, and they need a cheer-leader. That's where you come in. You, like the witnesses in Hebrews, have already run the laps they are just beginning. You're still running, of course, but many, many laps are under your belt. New college roommates, first dates, job interviews—been there, done that, haven't you?

So, now, cheer them on. Give them advice. Encourage them to stay strong. Support their activities. Two bits, four bits, six bits, a dollar—come on, Grandma, stand up and holler!

41

*Consistent, timely encouragement
has the staggering magnetic power
to draw an immortal soul to the
God of hope. The one whose name
is Wonderful Counselor.*

—Charles R. Swindoll

*Statistics aside, she had the desire to win. Everyone
was convinced she would be the state champion.*

A True Champion

"A champion is one who gets up when he can't." Those words were burned into Katelyn's mind as if someone had etched them in with a wood-burning kit at summer camp. The words were on a poster her grandmother had given her in the ninth grade. Katelyn had placed the poster at the foot of her bed, and for the past four years, she had started and ended her day with that challenge. How would Katelyn hold up when faced with a real challenge? Would she be a true champion?

There was no doubt in her grandmother's mind that she was. Grandma Jo had been there for her at every single track meet—all the way back to her second-grade track and field day. It didn't matter where the meet was held, Grandma Jo was always there. "Everybody's got to be somewhere," she would say. And Grandma Jo would hop in the car and drive two hours to Katelyn's school. Grandma Jo would sit up in the bleachers, wearing her big, floppy hat to shield her face from the sun. Grandma Jo had spent her teen years in southern California and never missed a chance to tell her grandchildren that too much sun was responsible for her wrinkles. She was the epitome of grace and poise—the dignified grandmother. At least until Katelyn reached the finish line. Then dignity and grace went out the window. She would jump for joy, hugging everyone in the stands. Next, she would run down to the track and give Katelyn the biggest hug, telling her she was so proud of her. She would say, "Katelyn, you have a gift! A gift to run."

And she was right. Running came easily to Katelyn. Like someone who sings with perfect pitch or plays the piano by ear, Katelyn could run. So she did. But as she got older, the coaches required more and more out of her. By the ninth grade, she was having to train after school and on weekends. Hours of running and weight training took the place of playing, practices crowded out parties, and healthy food replaced junk food.

After a particularly formidable workout on a day when the temperature was in the 90s, Katelyn called her grandmother. "Grandma Jo," she cried, "I wish God had given me a talent I didn't have to work so hard at!"

But Grandma Jo gently reminded her that God didn't have any talents like that. "We all have to work at whatever talent God gives us, or it will be taken away," she said. "Remember the parable of the talents?" Of course, Katelyn remembered the parable, but she had never thought of it like that.

A few days later, Katelyn received the poster in the mail that was to become her of symbol of strength. The poster showed six runners, each straining to be the first to reach the finish tape. Veins clearly being challenged, muscles pushed to a new level, and teeth clenched as each face revealed a passionate desire to win. It was just the challenge Katelyn needed. She set her sights higher, and her goals became clearer.

Blue ribbons, red ribbons, trophies, and medals began to fill her room. Victory after victory, her grandmother was there to congratulate and cheer her on. Time seemed to fly by until, one day during her senior year of high school, she found herself at the state track meet. All the hard work would pay off here.

Katelyn had run only hurdles for the past two years, but was seemingly made for the event. Statistically speaking, she was the district and regional champion and came into the state meet with the second fastest time. Statistics aside, she had the desire to win. Everyone was convinced she would be the state champion.

Every athlete has his or her pre-sport rituals. Katelyn was down on the track going through her predetermined set: Bounce three or four times, shake out arms and legs, touch toes, and then look into the crowd for support. There were her whole family— Mom, Dad, brothers, sisters, aunts, uncles, and of course, her Grandma Jo. She had driven nine hours to see this important event. She wouldn't have missed it for anything. It was late May in southern Louisiana, and the "track" hat, as Katelyn called it, was shading her face. She was poised and ready to hug and congratulate. She gave Katelyn one last wave for good luck.

Katelyn bent down to the spongy red track and spread her fingers out in precisely the same way she had done a hundred times. Then she placed her toes snugly into the starting block. She, like the crowd, waited for the familiar sound of the gun. Then the official yelled, "Everyone up!" Shaking out her arms and legs, Katelyn was determined to stay focused. Back down they all went. Every finger in the perfect spot, toes lined up, head lowered, Katelyn was ready. Once again, the official called for everyone to get up. Back up and once again, back down. Surely, the gun would go off this time. But it was not to be. Even the crowd was getting nervous as once again the official asked the runners to stand. This time he told Katelyn to move her block back. *What could be wrong?* Katelyn thought. It was where

she always put it. Although puzzled, she was ready for the race to begin, so she did as she was told. She felt an uneasy feeling in her stomach. She thought of her grandma's last wave, and she knew it meant "You can do it." So with new resolve, she calmly stretched out her fingers as if playing a piano piece at Christmas and waited. Finally, the sound of the gun. They were off. She had a great start and seemed to fly over the first hurdle. But her toe skimmed the second hurdle. The third hurdle shook as once again her foot lightly touched it. On the fourth hurdle, she was down. The crowd went instantly silent in disbelief. Katelyn felt their sadness for her as a dream had quickly died. The other runners flew past her. There was no reason for them to stop. Nobody blamed them.

Katelyn's knee was badly cut and her hands were burned from rubbing across the track. But she knew it

was time for the real test. Was her grandmother's poster to become a reality? Could she get up and complete this race? She began the long journey to the finish line. What usually took less than sixteen seconds seemed like an eternity. The audience applauded her determination as Katelyn made it to the finish line and quietly walked off the track. She knew there would be no medals, no articles in the paper, no congratulatory hugs. And she felt so sorry for those who had traveled so far— only to be disappointed. As she raised her head, there came her family with Grandma Jo leading the way. Everyone who had stood by her in victory now stood beside her in defeat.

But was it a defeat? Grandma Jo hadn't traveled nine hours just to see Katelyn win; she came to see her finish a race. And just like God, she was just as ready to wrap her arms around the runner who had hit a few hurdles, suffered some scrapes, and finished last as she was the runner who cleared every hurdle and finished first. As Grandma Jo tells the story, on that day, she saw a champion run a race, and Katelyn came to understand more clearly the love of God.

Tell the story of when you cheered on a grandchild during a challenging time.

_____

_____

_____

_____

_____

_____

_____

_____

_____

_____

_____

You Are a
Forever Student

Keep
Learning

Not even old age, wrinkles, or gray hairs can stop Me from sustaining you. Don't lose heart! Your external appearances may be fading away, but I'm renewing your spirit day by day. May you always speak with wisdom and faithful instruction.

Teaching you,
Your God of Wisdom

—from Isaiah 46:4; 2 Corinthians 4:16;
Proverbs 31:26

Chances are you haven't heard a school bell ring in years, but the shrill sound of any bell probably brings back memories of a small wooden desk and a teacher with a stern look. Do you ever wish the final bell would ring and school would be out forever?

The reality is that school is still in session, but you'll be happy to hear that you won't forever be waiting for a school bus or a carpool. And you can now pass up the clean, white notebooks and freshly sharpened pencils that complete the "Back to School" displays at Wal-Mart and Kmart. And the worries you had with locker combinations, lunch money, and best friends have discreetly faded just like the yearbook pages they are recorded on.

Yes, the physical description of your schoolroom has vastly changed, as well as the physical description of your teacher. But the opportunities to learn are ever present. Grandmothers, those opportunities will

present quite a challenge to you—you'll have
to apply yesterday's wisdom to today's challenges!
And who better to present those challenges to you
than your grandchildren?

You've lived long enough to realize that the best
teachers are not always those who are old and wise or
hold a fancy degree. Your grandchildren will supply you
with enough material to fill a three-ring binder with
five divider tabs. You've never had a professor who
could talk as fast as a four-year-old grandson or with as
much emotion as a twelve-year-old granddaughter.
They will gently remind you when hairstyles change
and rock groups go out of style. They will push you
harder than any P.E. teacher with words like "Run,
Grandma!" or "Can you still ride a bike?"

Yes, your grandchildren will be full of
valuable information and insight. Now,
what do you have to do? Just study hard
and try to pass their tests! You can do
it, Grandma!

Cheerfulness and contentment are great beautifiers and are famous preservers of good looks.

—Charles Dickens

Today was her birthday, and she planned to see a plastic surgeon on the following Thursday afternoon.

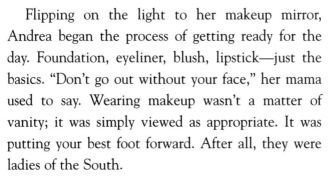

Wrinkles and Rainbows

Flipping on the light to her makeup mirror, Andrea began the process of getting ready for the day. Foundation, eyeliner, blush, lipstick—just the basics. "Don't go out without your face," her mama used to say. Wearing makeup wasn't a matter of vanity; it was simply viewed as appropriate. It was putting your best foot forward. After all, they were ladies of the South.

Southern women always looked their best: peaches-and-cream complexions; natural, but fixed hairstyles; casual, but elegant clothing—that's a true Southern lady. Andrea's grandchildren often teased her when she wore white linen to their ball games. "Why are you so dressed up, Mama Andrea?" But Andrea would tell them white linen is not dressed up, just comfortable.

Andrea was a "cute" grandmother. She had a youthful appearance that included a modern, short hairdo—not "old lady" hair—that framed a small, round face. And she was petite. Anybody petite is labeled "cute" from early on. She had gotten used to that description. What she hadn't gotten used to was the skin on her cheeks becoming droopy. She wasn't sure if the word *droopy* was the medical term, but it certainly was accurate.

Today was her birthday, and she planned to see a plastic surgeon on the following Thursday afternoon. She had decided that at sixty-five, she could do something about her "droopies." She was so nervous

about the appointment that it took her weeks to get the courage to make it. Several of her friends had used this particular doctor and were pleased with the results.

Wrinkles and Rainbows

As she sat in front of the makeup mirror, she moved the skin on her face around, trying to get a glimpse of what she might look like post-droopy. *What will Billy think about this?* she thought. *I wonder if he'll even notice.*

Billy was her first great-grandson, and every time she was with him, he would take his little fingers and pull the skin on her face. He did it so softly. It wasn't in any way a mean gesture. It was just his four-year-old way of touching and identifying her as his grandmother. *He probably won't notice. Anyway, this surgery is for me. Not anyone else. Just putting my best foot forward.*

Andrea finished her makeup session and headed to her closet to dress. She wasn't used to having so much time to dress and pamper herself. Her husband and children were doing all the cooking. She wasn't to do anything—her family had made that clear. No one wanted to celebrate at a restaurant, so the solution was for the family to share the cooking responsibilities. Andrea wanted to help, and would have been happy to, but they insisted.

You Are a Forever Student—*Keep Learning*

What do you wear to a birthday party when you're sixty-five years old? It seemed to Andrea that it was just yesterday that she was deciding what to wear to her sixth birthday. Her mama had wanted her to wear a fancy party dress with white patent leather shoes. She had wanted to wear a new pair of blue gingham shorts with a matching shirt. Her mama finally convinced her that the party dress was more appropriate. *I wonder what Mama would think of the clothes my grandchildren will wear tonight? No doubt there will be an assortment of blue jeans and shorts. They will be precious, and no one will care what they have on. The times are so different.*

Andrea carefully selected a blue linen skirt, a freshly ironed white blouse, and white sandals with tiny flowers across the toe. She did have blue jeans in her closet, and she wore them, but not for a birthday party.

The meal was delicious. Andrea was surprised at the assortment of meats. Her husband had prepared his speciality: chicken, beef, and ribs marinated all night then grilled to perfection. He had really worked hard to make the evening special. The vegetables, salads, and desserts were compliments of her two daughters and one daughter-in-law. No restaurant in town would have had better food. And it was so nice to relax at home and enjoy the family without the distraction of others. That was the best part.

As the sun set, Andrea found herself in her favorite spot doing one of her most favorite things—sitting on the porch swing with Billy. He was adorable. His curly hair had just recently gotten its first "big boy" haircut, and his big brown eyes looked up at her like a little puppy dog. Billy had a gentle spirit—there was no other way to describe him—he was just born with it. He was one of those kids who laughs at everything and loves everyone.

Billy was chattering about playing baseball in the backyard with his daddy; he'd been working hard to learn how to hit the ball. Next year he would be five and could play T-ball. Andrea delighted in hearing these stories and anything else Billy wanted to tell her. Billy was getting sleepy and had laid his head down in Andrea's lap. Andrea looked down and smiled at this precious child.

"Billy, I can't wait until your first game. I'm going to be right there cheering you on."

Billy stared intently at Andrea and then said, "Mama Andrea, when you smile, your face makes rainbows."

Andrea laughed out loud. "My face makes rainbows! Billy, I just thought it made wrinkles. How fun to think that it makes rainbows! Thank you for telling me that."

Later that evening, as Andrea retold the story to her husband, he wanted to know if she was going to cancel her doctor's appointment. Andrea stared in the mirror and thought, *No, but I will tell him to leave enough for a rainbow.*

*What fresh view on life have you learned
from your grandchildren?*

_____

_____

_____

_____

_____

_____

_____

_____

_____

_____

_____

You Have
a Secret

Share It

© Photography by Lamar

$\mathcal{I}$ ve searched you and know you. The secret things in life belong to Me! But the treasures I've revealed to you belong to you and your family to be passed down for generations. And be patient—I'm not finished with you yet! I'm still in the process of completing the good work I started in you.

Intimately,

Your Creator and God

—from Psalm 139:1;
Deuteronomy 29:29; Philippians 1:6

Has it ever been truer than today that grandmas come in all shapes and sizes? Like fresh fallen snowflakes that become a mountain of white, each grandmother is unique. Yes, some of you are still blonde, brunette, or redheaded, without a gray hair in sight (thanks, Clairol), and some retain a somewhat girlish figure (thanks, aerobics). More and more of us are still working outside the home, playing tennis, running in marathons, and climbing mountains.

But there are others who have slowed down a bit, acquired a beautiful head of white hair, and spend their time gardening, sewing, and canning. And there are many, many somewhere in-between. But, grandmas, while you may not look alike or act alike, there is one thing you all have in common: You are the mother of one of your grandchildren's parents. Oh, what a unique position that puts you in.

What childhood secrets are secured in your closets, drawers, and under your beds! You are the one who can look at your grandchild and say, "He acts just

like his father" or, "She is the spitting image of
her mother." And with this knowledge, you hold
the invaluable ability to link the past to the present.

It doesn't matter whether you're forty-four or
seventy-four, or whether you play golf on Saturdays or
put up peas. It doesn't matter whether you live next-
door or a thousand miles away. You hold the key—that
most important key that unlocks secrets of the past to
a wide-eyed child—a child who never thought of his or
her parents as children. Secrets that only someone
who was there could know. When you think about it,
Grandma, you, your husband, and God are the only
people in your grandchildren's lives who witnessed
the early years of their parents. And just as God,
who knows us so well, realizes that deeper
knowledge of a person brings understanding
and love, you must recognize the power you
hold to unite generations with a single
story. So tell some stories—remind your
children of their past, and let your
grandchildren know that we were
all young once.

I want future generations to remember my good advice, but most of all I want them to remember my love.

—Heather Whitestone

Each line and wrinkle represented a story in the life of this sometimes "aggravating" little woman.

Grandma Shack

"Mom, do I have to take her with me?" Jessica moaned through clenched teeth. "Every time she hears my keys jingle, she picks up her purse! I can't go anywhere without my grandmother!" Jessica had only been seven when her Grandma Shack moved in. At the time of the move, Grandma Shack wasn't feeble by any means. She wasn't sick. She wasn't really that old. There was just no point in her living alone. Nine years had passed, and she still wasn't that feeble or that old. And Jessica was right—she was always ready to go. But a sixteen-year-old with a new car doesn't want her grandmother riding shotgun everywhere she goes.

You Have a Secret—*Share It*

"Mom, how did she get to be sixty-eight and not get a driver's license?"

Jessica's mom knew this was hard on Jessica. Actually, it had been hard on the whole family. When her mother-in-law had come to live with them, Jo wanted to make her feel welcome. But she had her six children to consider. Three very active boys and three equally active girls seemed to occupy every available inch of their four-bedroom home. Adding on to their house wasn't an option, so Grandma Shack had to share a room with Jessica, who was the youngest. Now that the older girls were in college, Jessica had moved into their room. Jo knew that over the years, the living arrangement had worked out fine, but she now felt some relief knowing her youngest daughter finally had some privacy.

There was no denying that Grandma Shack wasn't

easy to live with. She was quick to lay down some ground rules as she rooted out her place in the family nine years earlier. "There will be limited baby-sitting," this strong-willed, tiny Indian woman had said. Jo could still picture her standing there—all four feet, eleven inches tall with stick-straight white hair and hands on her hips. "I raised my children; now you raise yours. And I won't clean up after anyone but myself. I did my share of that also. I don't mind sharing a room, but when my soap operas are on in the afternoon, I like it quiet."

Jo remembered how she joked to her husband, Luke, that Grandma Shack just might make them sign a contract. Once the move was complete, a trunk, a white wicker rocker, a small TV, and twenty shoeboxes with important papers now occupied one-half of Jessica's pink and white ruffled, little-girl bedroom. On more than one occasion, Jo wondered what she had gotten her family into.

"Jessica, just take her with you one more time. I'll talk to your daddy about her. Maybe he can talk to her about letting us know ahead of time when she needs an errand run," Jo pleaded with Jessica.

"Oh, all right," said Jessica. "Maybe I won't see anyone I know!"

"Grandma, I'm ready. Do you still need to pick up some things?" Jessica called down the hallway. There was not even a hint of disrespect in her voice. Jo and

You Have a Secret—*Share It*

Luke had been determined to raise their children to respect their elders, even if they weren't happy with them at the moment.

All the children knew Grandma had sacrificed so much to raise her family. Her life had not been easy. Jo had often thought that Grandma's face was truly a road map of her life. Each line and wrinkle represented a story in the life of this sometimes "aggravating" little woman. A woman who struggled to raise six children after leaving an alcoholic and abusive husband. *How did she endure so much? Losing a son in a motorcycle accident, sending the four remaining sons off one by one to fight a war, seeing that each child received a proper education—all the time wondering how to put food on the table. Thank you, God, that my life is easier than Grandma's was,* Jo prayed.

Grandma Shack quickly grabbed her purse and followed her granddaughter out the door. Jessica looked back at her mom and rolled her dark, brown eyes. Jo whispered a soft thank-you to her youngest daughter and thought that Jessica really had great patience for a sixteen-year-old. Years of sharing a room with a grandmother probably contributed to that.

Grandma Shack

As Grandma put her seat belt on, Jessica adjusted the mirror and began backing out of the long driveway. "Where do you need to go today, Grandma?" Jessica asked.

"Well, I need a little prune juice, and then I wanted to pick up a card for your daddy's birthday," was the reply. "You know, there was a time when I couldn't even afford a card for your daddy's birthday."

Oh no, thought Jessica, *not another story of how she raised six children with no husband around to help and how she worked in the school cafeteria to support them all.*

Jessica had heard those stories her whole life, and she really did sympathize with her, but did she have to hear them again today? Still she responded politely, "Yes, Grandma, I remember you telling me about those tough years. You really have some great stories. But why don't we talk about *today*."

Just then a car pulled out in front of Jessica. She slammed on her brakes, but there was no way she could stop soon enough. Jessica could hear the screeching of the tires and then the crunch of metal as the two cars collided.

Then she realized that even though she had hit the car, they were still moving. She reached up and put the car in park and it jolted to a stop. Jessica felt her head lunge forward, and her chin hit hard against the steering wheel.

"Jessica, are you okay?" Grandma Shack was yelling. Jessica felt something on her chin and realized it was blood, but she was okay.

"I'm fine, Grandma, what about you?"

"I think so. Just shaken up," she responded.

"Grandma, I can't open my door. I'm getting scared," Jessica cried.

"You're okay. I already hear a police car. Just hang on a minute." Grandma reassured her. Grandma was right. Jessica could hear a siren getting louder and louder.

"Grandma, I'm praying that God will help us get

out of this wreck. And when we do, I promise I'll listen to any story you want to tell me about the old days."

The doctors and nurses were so nice at the emergency room. Jessica's teeth had gone through her chin as she hit the steering wheel, and that required several stitches. X-rays were taken and closely reviewed. Jessica and Grandma had pulled some muscles, but no bones were broken.

Friends and family poured into their house all that evening expressing concern and love. Grandma Shack and Jessica sat side by side, telling their story together. Jessica would begin with what road they were on and how scared she was when she looked up and saw the car pull out in front of them. Grandma would finish the story telling about Jessica's prayer and promise to listen to her stories. Everyone laughed as Grandma held Jessica's hand and told her she planned to hold her to that promise.

Later that night, after all the visitors left, Grandma and Jessica found that they were more than exhausted. They were also pretty sore. Jessica got her pajamas on and peeked into her old room where Grandma Shack had already climbed into the twin bed she had slept in for the last nine years. She looked over at this old woman who had shared her room for so many years. *Funny, what a difference a day makes!*

You Have a Secret—*Share It*

"Grandma, do you mind if I sleep in your room tonight?" Jessica asked.

"Of course not, Jessica. What's on your mind?" Grandma asked.

"I was just thinking how much I appreciate you and the sacrifices you made for your family. And how much you helped me today. Encouraging me to stay calm when I was really scared. There were probably lots of times when you were really scared and there was no one to help you. I just thought you might need me to sleep next to you tonight."

"I think that would be great," Grandma said. "I would love to have someone sleep near me tonight."

"Grandma, now that it's all over and we're okay," Jessica said in a sleepy voice, "I was just thinking how I can't wait to tell my grandchildren the story that we share together. It's a pretty good one, isn't it?"

Record a story here that is worth passing on.

_____

_____

_____

_____

_____

_____

_____

_____

_____

_____

_____

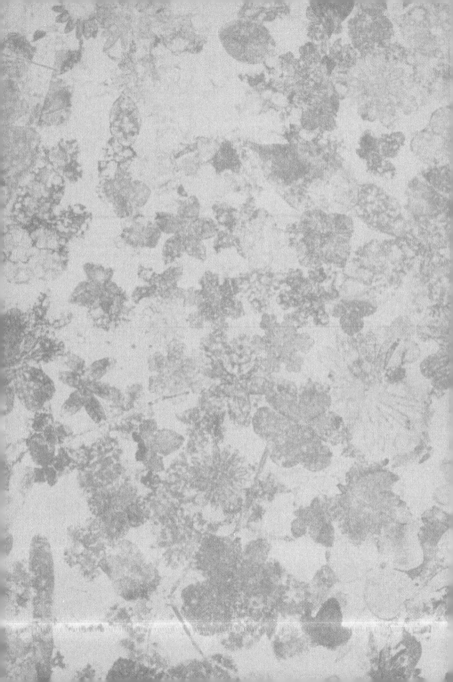

You Are a
Preserver of the Past

Preserve It

$\mathcal{R}$emember the treasured traditions your ancestors have passed down to you. Reflect on your own cherished memories as you consider all the ways I've worked in your life. Share your sincere heritage of faith with your family for generations to come. Tell them of the days gone by and all My marvelous works. Your children and grandchildren applaud you and call you blessed.

Love,
Your Rock of Ages

—from Deuteronomy 32:7; 2 Timothy 1:5–6; Psalm 143:5; Proverbs 31:28

Tradition! Who can say that word without hearing the booming voice of Tevye from *Fiddler on the Roof*? Tevye was challenged with the dilemma of accepting new ways that seemed to interfere with what was traditionally accepted. What should he do? How could he mix the old with the new?

More importantly, what should you do, Grandma? You, like Tevye, have to be a defender and preserver of tradition! The minute you become a grandmother, it becomes your responsibility to polish all family traditions and to prepare them for passage. Traditions are those important things that should be passed from one generation to another because tradition says that you are connected!

But we live in a very mobile society, and it isn't easy to keep traditions alive. Many would even argue against the value of tradition, stating that "times have changed." But no one will ever convince *you* that just because we have computers, a grandma with a good book has become obsolete or that a grandma's home cooking for Sunday lunch isn't the best meal in town just because we have restaurants on every corner. Just because families sometimes live clear across America from each other doesn't mean the highways won't continue to wear down from cars headed to Grandma's house every holiday. And just because we live in a time of "new" thinking doesn't mean that the "old" values of love, respect, honor, discipline, and dignity are out of date.

It's not that you don't like the new or don't welcome change. Who wants to go back to an icebox and candlelight? You love the new but want the best of the past to stay around awhile. And who can blame you?

So, Grandma, you keep on preserving and defending the traditions that make your family special. And never miss the opportunity to pass on something very important that was once passed on to you! If you ever stop, society will lose something very precious.

You will find, as you look back
upon your life, that the moments
when you have really lived are the
moments you have done things in
the spirit of love.

—Henry Drummond

This year, Mama Sue had decided that there would be no gingerbread house.

The Gingerbread House

"Christmas is for kids," the song by the country group, Alabama, played discreetly in the background. "Mama Sue," as her grandchildren called her, loved that song and believed it to be true. "Christmas is for kids," she sighed, exhausted from the long day of decorating. Mama Sue settled into her "grandma" chair for an evening of television and reading. Stockings that had weathered almost fifty Christmases hung once again over the fireplace, twinkle lights sparkled on a freshly cut tree, and colorful presents, carefully wrapped, completed the festive scene. Every house in Stillwater, Oklahoma, where she had lived for nearly seventy years, had a variety of stockings, lights, and presents.

Mama Sue knew that what had always set her house apart from the rest of Stillwater was her home-baked, meticulously decorated gingerbread houses. Red and green gumdrops lined the walls, white icing dripped from the roof, and candy canes carefully guarded the door. It was a child's dream house. One could almost picture a little elf peeking through the window, waiting for the night so he could come out and play. And when the gingerbread house was lovingly placed in the center of the dining room table, Christmas had officially arrived.

But this year, Mama Sue had decided that there would be no gingerbread house. Eventually all traditions die, she had reasoned.

"Christmas is for kids," the chorus rang out once

again. *But where are the kids?* she sadly thought. *I guess time marches on.* Her son and his family were almost two hours away. Her daughter lived in nearby Stillwater, but she was busy tonight with her own family projects.

The Gingerbread House

Mama Sue knew they would all come over sometime during the holidays, but for the most part, the daily hustle and bustle of Christmas no longer affected her, and sometimes she missed it!

Some of it, of course, she didn't miss. The long lines at department stores. The kids' endless questions about Santa. The bills following the holiday season. But the kids, with rosy cheeks and sparkling eyes—those she missed. Especially Josh. There's something special, something unexplainable, something almost magical about that first grandchild. Maybe it's that just when you think you've reached a point in your life where maybe you're not so *needed*, you find yourself bound by the needs of a grandchild.

Josh certainly had fulfilled every grandmother's dream. Beautiful blue eyes, kind, gentle manners, strong and athletic, Josh was the first of eight beautiful grandchildren. She adored them all. But still, there's something special about the first.

The making of the gingerbread house began the year Josh was born. There's no denying that all the children loved it, but, for Josh, it truly was the symbol of Christmas. This would be Josh's first Christmas away from home. On December 22, he had married a beautiful girl from Louisiana. They had planned a two-day honeymoon to San Antonio and then Christmas would be spent with her family. Oklahoma was just too far to travel in that short amount of time. Of course, this was part of Mama Sue's decision not to make the gingerbread house. "I was there for the wedding, and it was great to spend time with him and to meet Ashley," she told herself. "He has better things to think about this Christmas than a silly old gingerbread house!"

As Mama Sue reached for the remote to see if *Touched by an Angel* had started, a soft voice seemed to say, "Where's the gingerbread house?" She tried to shake away the feeling as she flipped through the channels, but once again, from somewhere unknown, a little voice that strangely sounded like Josh's asked, "Where's the gingerbread house?"

"I'm tired," she announced out loud, as if to reaffirm to herself and the little voice that she truly was tired. After all, she hadn't fully recovered from that trip to Louisiana.

"Where's the gingerbread house?" the little voice nagged.

"That's it," she said. "What is this power grandchildren have over us?" Putting down the remote and pushing down the footrest, Mama Sue declared, "It's not Christmas yet!"

With experienced hands and a grandmother's heart, the construction began. From walls to roof, this seemed to be the best house ever. As she placed the last gumdrop on the chimney, Mama Sue thought, *I wish I could see Josh's face when he opens the box.* But she could picture his face. She knew exactly what it would look like.

He would open the box, and a smile that could sell even bad toothpaste would light up his face. And, those eyes, as clear blue as the sky, would be almost closed as if his face could hold no more than the smile. What a gift he had been to her all these years! "I guess it's time for me to share Josh and my gingerbread house with others," she said. Off to the bedroom to find the sturdiest box she

had, Mama Sue now felt a sense of urgency. "This is going to have to go out overnight express!"

It was the morning of Christmas Eve. Josh and Ashley were excited about their first Christmas together. The doorbell rang and Josh eagerly jumped up to see who had come to visit. After a few minutes, Josh declared, "Honey, it's Christmas!"

"I know," Ashley yelled back from the back room of their new house.

"No," said Josh, as he delicately placed the gingerbread house on their dining room table, "I mean, it's officially Christmas!"

Reflect on a special family tradition that you have helped to preserve.

_____

_____

_____

_____

_____

_____

_____

_____

_____

_____

_____

You Are Hope

Keep It Up

*H*ope in My good name! As you trust in Me, I'll fill you with all joy and peace, flooding your life with hope. Remember, your face reflects My glory. Even better, you're being transformed into My likeness with an ever-increasing glory. Surely My goodness and mercy will follow you and your family each and every day of your lives.

Making all things possible,

Your God of All Hope

—from Psalm 52:9; Romans 15:13;
2 Corinthians 3:18; Psalm 23:6; Matthew 19:26

Grandmothers, you are a model of hope to the young. *Hope* means to long for, to anticipate, to envision. Although you dreamed some dreams that never came true, set some goals that were never met, and had some ideas that never became reality, your grandchildren do not know that. They see dreams coming true when they attend a celebration honoring your many years of marriage. They see goals accomplished when someone hands you a gift in recognition of a job well done at a retirement party. They see your ideas become a reality when upon their graduation you present to them a quilt you've lovingly crafted.

You are the hope for a world of young people who are afraid to dream for fear their dreams won't come true. We look at a new baby and declare he or she is our hope for the future. And it's true. But hasn't the hope for tomorrow always depended upon the accomplishments of yesterday? The success and strength of America has always depended on the success and strength of our forefathers.

inspirational message

The same is true with your grandchildren. Their future depends in large on your past. Your decisions, your dreams, your accomplishments are really the beginning of their lives. The most obvious decision affecting their very being was your choice of a life mate. Perhaps where they live now was also your decision many years ago. And perhaps even your job choices have affected your grandchildren. There are many families where "following in Grandma's foot-steps" has produced teachers, nurses, or company presidents.

More important, you made a decision to live as a believer of Jesus, and now they have the chance to follow that path also. What a great connection! Just as God gives hope to a lost and dying world, you are a "hope-giver." Isn't it amazing to real-ize that many years after you are gone, you will live on! The strength of your past is the future of your grandchildren. And you're not through yet—keep up the good work!

You are God's workmanship,
a quilt of beauty to behold.

—Karla Dornacher

She had recently become a card-carrying member of the "sandwich club."

A Little Girl with a Grandma Face

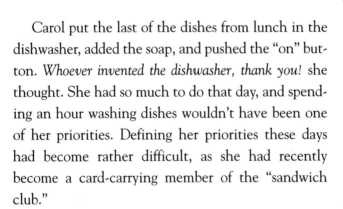

Carol put the last of the dishes from lunch in the dishwasher, added the soap, and pushed the "on" button. *Whoever invented the dishwasher, thank you!* she thought. She had so much to do that day, and spending an hour washing dishes wouldn't have been one of her priorities. Defining her priorities these days had become rather difficult, as she had recently become a card-carrying member of the "sandwich club."

The "sandwich club" was the term used to refer to people who were caring for their aging parents as well as their own children. "Sandwiched between two generations" was the way the article had described Carol's stage of life. More than once in the last few years, Carol had scoured magazines for articles on caring for an aging parent just as she had scoured magazines about pregnancy many years ago. She really couldn't believe how much information was available on the topic of aging. *Has there always been this much written about aging,* Carol wondered, *and I just didn't notice because it didn't affect me?* She couldn't help but wonder how many times she may not have noticed others who were facing the "sandwich" dilemma, never bothering to offer help or an encouraging word. *Well, now I know, and I promise to be more alert to others in the future.*

Carol had a bonus—maybe her situation was a "sandwich, with the extras"—she now had grandchildren. Her oldest daughter was married with two children,  while her youngest daughter was a teenager still at home. Carol's priorities came from whoever needed her the most. On most days, she struggled with how to face toddlers, teens, and the elderly with equal enthusiasm. "I can do all things through Christ who strengthens me" was Carol's new favorite verse, and she quoted it often.

It wasn't as if she would change anything even if she could. When her mother began to have trouble functioning in her own house, Carol never questioned whether her mother would move in with her. And when her daughter needed help with her children, she always wanted to be there for her. And, of course, the demands of an active teenager with sports and school plays were ever present, and Carol was happy to be asked to help in whatever way she could. That's just the way she was raised. Family came first. But on some days, she was definitely ready for "Calgon" to take her away.

Tossing the dirty dishtowel on the washing machine, she leaned over to pick up a roller skate that had made its way into the kitchen. The skate reminded her that she needed to check on the grandkids. They were in the living room playing with "Me-maw." Me-maw was the grandmother name all the kids called her mother. Entering the room, Carol found Me-maw on the floor playing with her great-grandchildren. Carol's daughter, Chrissy, had left her six-year-old daughter, Korie, and four-year-old son, Ryan, with her while she ran some errands. *If things were normal*, Carol thought, *I wouldn't have to look in on the kids while they played with Me-maw.*

But things were not normal and hadn't been for two years now. That's when the thief—as Carol called it—had entered her mother's home. That's when Me-maw was diagnosed with Alzheimer's disease. Carol had shared with her father that Alzheimer's was like a thief because it robbed her mother of so many things. Her command of language was gone, as well as her memory of all the years they had shared together. She now spoke in fragmented sentences and would forget events that happened just minutes before. And Carol knew that as time went on, her words and her memory would disappear entirely.

Carol had wanted her mother to stay in her own home in familiar surroundings as long as possible, but Carol had gradually begun to notice how difficult it was for her father to take care of her mother. When Carol would go over to check on them, she would find the cereal in the dishwasher and the milk in a cabinet. Finally, the time came to move them in with her.

A Little Girl with a Grandma Face

Looking at her mom, playing peacefully with the children, Carol knew that if Alzheimer's hadn't come into Me-maw's life, she would have been up cooking and cleaning and listening to one of her favorite gospel music groups on the radio—singing along in her beautiful alto voice.

Carol was instantly grateful she had inherited her mother's voice and her blue eyes. *A constant reminder of what she once was*, Carol thought. But then Carol knew there were other reminders too: Me-Maw's recipes she cooked for her own family and friends; phrases she said to her children; clothes she made using Me-maw's patterns; and quilts, casually thrown over beds and chairs, that had been pieced together by Me-maw's loving hands. Carol realized and was grateful that while the thief took her mother's memory, he had not taken hers. That's where Me-maw would live now and forever—in Carol's heart and mind. And Carol would pass that memory on to her children and grandchildren.

Everything changes when Alzheimer's enters your family. But life goes on, doesn't

it? Carol had half expected things to stand still as she cared for her mom, but she was so glad they hadn't. She knew that the seemingly small, insignificant, everyday events of life would help her get through the next few years. And seeing her grandchildren playing with Me-maw was one of those seemingly insignificant but extremely important events of this particular day. A memory had just been made. *Thank you, God, for this day and for this memory I'll always have of my mother.*

"Hey, Mom!" Chrissy said cheerfully as she walked into the living room, shaking Carol out of her thoughtful trance. "I got so much done today. Thanks for watching the kids. I don't know what I would do without you and Me-maw. Okay, kiddos, are you ready to go home?"

"Mom," said Korie, whose long curly hair had shaken free of the ponytail holder and now fell halfway down her back, "we've had the best time. We played Barbies and drew pictures, and we went out back and picked up pecans. I think Me-maw's just like a little girl, only she has a grandma face!"

A Little Girl with a Grandma Face

Tears came to Carol's eyes as she realized that her grandchildren were also forming memories. They weren't the same memories Carol had, for they were making their own. And as they grew older, Carol would be happy to add her memories of Me-maw to theirs.

What strengths from your past are becoming the future of your grandchildren?

_____

_____

_____

_____

_____

_____

_____

_____

_____

_____